Divine Design for LEADERS
you are formed for a purpose

gifts ▪ passion ▪ personality

DR. MICHALE AYERS

Copyright © 2013 by Michale R. Ayers
All rights reserved.
ISBN: 1490429379
ISBN-13: 978-1490429373

Worksheets in this booklet are copyrighted materials.
Assessments, profiles, and pages herein are
not to be copied without permission of the author.
Students and participants in classes where this
material is taught must purchase individual workbooks.

The Piece of Puzzle:

- Each piece is _____.
- Each is _____ for a purpose.
- Each finds _____ only as it FITS with the big picture.
- The piece is incomplete without the _____ picture.
- The picture is _____ without the individual piece.

The Big Picture:

Examine: _____

1 Corinthians 10:12-27

The body is a unit, though it is made up of many parts; and though all its parts are many, they form one body. So it is with Christ. For we were all baptized by one Spirit into one body—whether Jews or Greeks, slave or free—and we were all given the one Spirit to drink.

Now the body is not made up of one part but of many. If the foot should say, "Because I am not a hand, I do not belong to the body," it would not for that reason cease to be part of the body. And if the ear should say, "Because I am not an eye, I do not belong to the body," it would not for that reason cease to be part of the body. If the whole body were an eye, where would the sense of hearing be? If the whole body were an ear, where would the sense of smell be? But in fact God has arranged the parts in the body, every one of them, just as he wanted them to be. If they were all one part, where would the body be? As it is, there are many parts, but one body.

The eye cannot say to the hand, "I don't need you!" And the head cannot say to the feet, "I don't need you!" On the contrary, those parts of the body that seem to be weaker are indispensable, and the parts that we think are less honorable we treat with special honor. And the parts that are unpresentable are treated with special modesty, while our presentable parts need no special treatment. But God has combined the members of the body and has given greater honor to the parts that lacked it, so that there should be no division in the body, but that its parts should have equal concern for each other. If one part suffers, every part suffers with it; if one part is honored, every part rejoices with it.

Now you are the body of Christ, and each one of you is a part of it.

(1 Corinthians 10:12-17, NIV)

Apply:

As a group discuss what Paul's analogy of the body of Christ means for the church today…

Live:

As an individual, what might this mean for you? What changes should you consider making?

Section One: Spiritual Gifts

MY MINISTRY IS DETERMINED BY _____.

The BEING – DOING Equation:

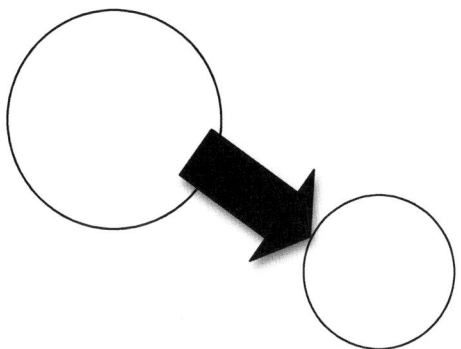

- What I do should flow from _____

<u>What God made me to BE determines what He intends for me to Do</u>. I will understand the purpose I was created for when I understand the kind of person I am. This is the secret of knowing God's will for my life- and discovering how to function in life, relationships and ministry.

God is consistent in his plan for each of our lives. He would not give us personalities, passions and gifts and then not use them in our lives.

The two results of discovering the ministry I've been formed for are:

_____ and _____

HOW HAS GOD DESIGNED ME?

Examine:

"For we are God's workmanship, created in Christ Jesus to do good works, which God prepared in advance for us to do." Ephesians 2:10, NIV

God has been molding and shaping you for ministry since you were born. In fact, God started uniquely shaping you even before you were born!

Psalm 139:14-16 (NIV)

14 I praise you because I am fearfully and wonderfully made;
   your works are wonderful,
   I know that full well.

15 My frame was not hidden from you
   when I was made in the secret place.
   When I was woven together in the depths of the earth,

16 your eyes saw my unformed body.
   All the days ordained for me
   were written in your book
   before one of them came to be.

Apply:

THIS PASSAGE TELLS US...

1. I was _____ for a purpose.

2. I am _____!

3. I am _____!

KEY TRUTH: In ministry...Function follows Form!

Live: _____

"There are different kinds of gifts, but the same Spirit. There are different kinds of service, but the same Lord. There are different kinds of working, but the same God works all of them in all men. Now to each one the manifestation of the Spirit is given for the common good." (I Cor. 12:4-7, NIV)

THE DIVINE DESIGN INDEX:

gifts
spiritual gifts
1 Cor. 10 - 13

passions
calling, vision, heart
Galatians 2:8; Acts 16:9-10,

personality
temperament traits
Examples: Paul, Peter, Barnabus

G _____
"And of this gospel I was appointed a preacher and an apostle and a teacher".
2 Tim. 1:11, NASB

WHAT AM I GIFTED TO DO?

P _____
"It has always been my ambition to preach the gospel where Christ was not known…" Romans 15:20, NIV

"For God, who was at work in the ministry of Peter as an apostle to the Jews, was also at work in my ministry as an apostle to the Gentiles." Galatians 2:8, NIV

WHAT AM I PASSIONATE ABOUT DOING?

P_____

"For you have heard of my previous way of life in Judaism, how intensely I persecuted the church of God and tried to destroy it. 14I was advancing in Judaism beyond many Jews of my own age and was extremely zealous for the traditions of my fathers." Galatians 1:13-14, NIV

WHERE DOES MY PERSONALITY BEST SUIT ME TO SERVE?

Your ministry will be most fruitful and fulfilling when you are using your GIFTS in the area of your PASSIONS, and in a way that best expresses your PERSONALITY!

SUCCESS IN LIFE IS ONE THING:

_____

WHAT THE BIBLE SAYS ABOUT SPIRITUAL GIFTS

"Now about spiritual gifts I do not want you to be ignorant..."
1 Cor. 12:1, NIV

Examine: _____

A SPIRITUAL GIFT:

A special _____, given by the _____ to every _____ at their conversion, to be used to _____ to others and therefore to build up the body of Christ.

TEN TRUTHS:

1. Only _____ have spiritual gifts. (1 Cor. 2:14)

2. Every Christian has at least _____ gift. (1 Cor. 12:27-30)

3. No one receives _____ the gifts. (1Cor. 12:11)

4. No single gift is given to _____ (1 Cor. 12:29-30)

5. You can't _____ for a spiritual gift.
   (Eph. 4:7)

6. The _____ decides what gifts I get.
   (1 Cor. 12:11)

7. The gifts I'm given are _____.
   (Rom. 11:29)

8. I am to _____ the gifts God gives me.
   (1 Tim. 4:14)

9. It's a sin to _____ the gifts God gives me.
   (1 Cor. 4:1-2; Matthew 25:14-30)

10. Using my gifts _____ God and _____ me. (John 15:8)

Apply: _____

THE PURPOSE OF SPIRITUAL GIFTS

A. NOT FOR MY BENEFIT, BUT _____.
"Each one should use whatever gift he has received to serve others, faithfully administering God's grace in its various forms." 1 Peter 4:10, NIV

"Now to each one the manifestation of the Spirit is given for the common good."
1 Cor. 12:7, NIV

B. TO PRODUCE _____ AND _____ IN OUR CHURCH FAMILY.

"It was he who gave some to be apostles, some to be prophets, some to be evangelists, and some to be pastors and teachers, to prepare God's people for works of service, so that the body of Christ may be built up until we all reach unity in the faith and in the knowledge of the Son of God and become mature, attaining to the whole measure of the fullness of Christ...."
Ephesians 4:11-14

CAUTIONS ABOUT SPIRITUAL GIFTS

1. Don't confuse gifts with natural talents

2. Don't confuse gifts with the Fruit of the Spirit. (Gal. 5:22-23)

    -"Fruit" shows may Maturity
    -"Gifts" show my Ministry

3. Be aware of the "gift projection" tendency (i.e. expecting others to serve the way you do and have similar results).

4. Don't feel my gift makes me superior to others. (1 Cor. 12:21)

5. Realize that using my gift without love is worthless!
    "If I speak in the tongues of men and of angels, but have not love, I am only a resounding gong or a clanging cymbal. If I have the gift of prophecy and can fathom all mysteries and all knowledge, and if I have a faith that can move mountains, but have not love, I am nothing. If I give all I possess to the poor and surrender my body to the flames, but have not love, I gain nothing." 1 Cor. 13:1-3, NIV

6. Understand the difference between a spiritual gift and the responsibilities that every believer has. For instance, although there is a spiritual gift of giving, every believer should give:

    "On the first day of every week, <u>each one of you</u> should set aside a sum of money in keeping with his income, saving it up, so that when I come no collections will have to be made." 1 Corinthians 16:2, NIV

* Spiritual gifts mean that people who possess these gifts will be much more passionate, fulfilled and fruitful in the exercise of their gift. This goes above and beyond the responsibilities and blessings each of us have in Christ.

Live: _____

HOW TO DISCOVER YOUR GIFT (START)

S_____
Understand the Bible's teaching about gifts

T_____
Experiment with different areas of service

A_____
Use the "Spiritual Gift Assessment" Tool

R_____
Ask others what gifts they see in you

T_____
Get involved in ministry. Don't wait. If you wait you delay God's blessing, your fulfillment and cause your gifts to be undeveloped.

The Spiritual Gifts Assessment:

REMEMBER:

1. Have fun! These are not "tests"! There is no right or wrong answer. The purpose is to show how you are a unique blend!

2. Be honest. Don't put down what you hope or what you'd prefer to see in yourself. Put down what is true about yourself right now.

3. Each one is self-evaluation. No one is "rating" you on this. We're interested in your opinions about yourself, not what others. However it may be helpful to ask for additional input from those closest to you after you've filled in your own responses.

4. The value of each of these tools will vary depending on your age, how long you've been a Christian, your background, your honesty, and how much time and serious thinking you're willing to invest in them!

5. As you complete each tool, transfer your results to the form called "My Ministry Profile". You will bring this profile with you to your interview with a ministry director.

* This particular spiritual gift assessment tool does not include all the spiritual gifts. Some gifts are more self-evident than others. The explanation to come after the assessment clarifies ALL the gifts and helps you clarify whether you possess gifts not included in this assessment.

SPIRITUAL GIFT ASSESSMENT

You are about to undertake an exciting spiritual exercise. God has given you one or more spiritual gifts if you are a Christian, and discovering those gifts can be a thrilling experience.

You will be asked to answer the 104 questions listed below> Respond to each statement indicating the degree to which it is true of you.

    3-Almost always, consistently
    2-Often, much of the time
    1-Seldom, once in a while
    0-Rarely, never

IMPORTANT: Answer according to who you honestly are right now, not how you would like to be, or how you think you ought to be.

STEP ONE-Read each statement and mark each one indicating the degree to which the statement is true of you. Enter 0, 1, 2, or 3.

1. ____ I feel responsible to confront others with the truth of the gospel.

2. ____ I seek out unbelievers so I can present the message of Christ to them.

3. ____ I have compassion and I eagerly help people whom are hurting.

4. ____ I enjoy patiently, but firmly, nurturing others in their development as children of God.

5. ____ I am quick to lend a helping hand wherever needed.

6. ____ Because I want to see significant things happen for God's glory, I give more than a tithe.

7. ____ I appreciate each guest that comes into my home.

8. ____ I enjoy researching truth and effectively communicating it to others at their level.

9. ____ I enjoy strengthening the weak and reassuring the uncertain and unstable.

10. ____ I have unusual insight to give practical and godly advice to others.

11. ____ I willingly accept responsibility for leading groups that lack direction or leadership.

12. ____ I am careful, thorough, and skilled in details.

13. ____ I find it easy to believe that God will do amazing things if we trust him.

14. ____ I speak the truth of even when it is unpopular and difficult for others to accept.

15. ____ I strongly desire to share my faith with those apart from God.

16. ____ I readily gain the confidence of people in need.

17. ____ I prefer long term relationships in which I can model servant leadership for new and young believers.

18. ____ My difficulty is saying "NO" often results in over-involvement.

19. ____ I find fulfillment in sharing my money and possessions without expecting anything in return.

20. ____ I am more concerned with making a person feel comfortable and "safe" than I am about making an impression.

21. ____ I am able to study, understand, and share truth from God's Word.

22. ____ I can spontaneously discern needs and encourage people in the trenches.

23. ____ People find me approachable and comfortable to be with.

24. ____ I usually know where I am going and can influence people in that direction.

25. ____ I like to clarify goals and develop strategies to accomplish them.

26. ____ People come to me often for encouragement to trust God and believe His promises.

27. ____ I am willing to experience personal repentance and prompt repentance in others by sharing truth with them.

28. ____ Often when I share my faith or my church, people desire to know more and seek more information.

29. ____ I am more moved to alleviate the causes of people's hurts than to look for the benefits of the pain.

30. ____ I have compassion for people in our church and have a desire to lead and protect them.

31. ____ I am drawn to visible, tangible needs or projects that I can meet myself.

32. ____ I manage my money sell so that I can support people in need or ministries, which are important to me.

33. ____ I enjoy creating an environment for people to laugh and fellowship.

34. ____ I enjoy studying the Bible in order to present truth in an organized manner.

35. ____ I am willing and able to challenge or rebuke in order to encourage personal growth.

36. ____ I am compassionate, tolerant and able to discern people's needs.

37. ____ I am able to motivate others toward a goal.

38. ____ I feel frustrated an impatient when I see disorganization.

39. ____ Rarely do I struggle with believing God at His Word.

40. ____ My greatest joy is to announce the truth boldly to a specific situation.

41. ____ I am so concerned for the unchurched that I constantly feel motivated to invite people to church.

42. ____ I am able to empathize with suffering people and involve myself in their healing process.

43. ____ I am compelled to lead by example and let my life serve as a model.

44. ____ I would rather be supportive person than a "performer" up in front.

45. ____ I often give anonymously to help meet an individual or ministry's financial needs.

46. ____ I am attracted to, and enjoy, new people in the church.

47. ____ I challenge others to understand truth and obey it.

48. ____ I gravitate toward those who are confused or troubled in order to encourage them.

49. ____ I am very concerned about people's relational health and wholeness.

50. ____ I don't mind feeling alone in certain needed decisions.

51. ____ I am effective at organizing people as well as resources to meet goals, which the group has adopted.

52. ____ I can envision God's work and I readily believe that He will provide for this church.

53. ____ I feel a keen sense of responsibility to proclaim God's truth to people.

54. ____ My conversations with unbelievers often seem to include spiritual matters or church.

55. ____ I enjoy ministering to people in hospitals, prisons, and nursing homes.

56. ____ I am willing to spend much time caring for and nurturing a group of people.

57. ____ I am willing to tackle unglamorous jobs others neglect or consider unimportant.

58. ____ When I know that the money I share with others is truly needed, I don't worry about whether it will be replenished.

59. ____ I receive great satisfaction from working on social events that promote fellowship in the church.

60. ____ I can communicate difficult Biblical concepts in such a way that people become motivated to learn and study them more.

61. ____ I gently but firmly challenge others to greater obedience and self-discipline.

62. ____ I seek to restore the confused and brokenhearted.

63. ____ I am able to live with disagreement.

64. ____ I am able to devise effective plans to help a group meet specific objectives.

65. ____ I find it easy to venture into adventures that God has for me.

66. ____ I easily confront sin that I see in others or in the world.

67. ____ I look for and get excited about new ways to share my faith with others.

68. ____ I can easily look beyond a person's handicaps or their lingering problems to see a life that matters to God.

69. ____ I am willing to renounce personal interests for the sake of others.

70. ____ I enjoy doing things for others without being asked to do so.

71. ____ It is fulfilling to me to know that my financial support makes a difference in the lives and ministries of the church.

72. _____ I have a way of making strangers feel welcome and at ease.

73. _____ When I teach others, I feel comfortable responding to difficult questions.

74. _____ I reassure those who need to take courageous steps in their fait, family or life.

75. _____ I have excellent listening skills

76. _____ I have the vision and confidence needed to provide practical direction for groups within the church.

77. _____ I like the responsibility of coordinating the gifts and abilities of people who are working together for a common goal.

78. _____ I naturally risk knowing and believing that God will provide.

79. _____ I feel compelled to expose sin in the culture, church or an individual's life in order to help people walk consistently in truth.

80. _____ I am committed to seeing new believers become growing members of the body of Christ.

81. _____ I do what I can behind the scenes to show God's love to those who are suffering.

82. _____ I enjoy having responsibility for the growth of a group of Christians.

83. _____ I am content to work on "low profile" jobs where I see a need.

84. _____ I am concerned and careful about being faithful in issues of money management.

85. _____ I enjoy graciously providing food or lodging to those in need.

86. _____ I love to explain truth in a way that causes people to listen and act accordingly.

87. _____ I strengthen those who are wavering in their faith.

88. _____ In conversation, others say to me, "I never thought about it that way."

89. _____ When I am in a group, the other people look to me to take charge.

90. _____ I am able to visualize resources for ministry and bring them together to accomplish tasks related to that ministry.

91. _____ I find it easy to jump into adventures that God has for me.

92. _____ I can bring about conviction and change in the lives of others.

93. _____ I look for opportunities to build relationships with non-churched people.

94. ____ I help those who are unsupported and thought to be undeserving by others.

95. ____ I sacrificially give of myself for people under my responsibility.

96. ____ I enjoy meeting the needs of people or the church no matter what needs to be done.

97. ____ I like giving quietly behind the scenes without any public notice.

98. ____ I feel strongly about, using my home as an extension of my church's ministry.

99. ____ I have the desire and ability to relate truth to life so that people develop healthy attitudes and values.

100. ____ I inspire others to take the lordship of Christ more seriously.

101. ____ I can affirm, challenge and discipline others in love.

102. ____ My natural tendency when I see an unstructured situation is to jump in and take the lead.

103. ____ I can handle many details at one time in order to accomplish a task.

104. ____ I find it easy to follow God without knowing all the details of His Will in advance.

(Proceed to Step 2 on next page)

STEP TWO – transfer the numbers for all of the statements to "Spiritual Gifts Response Sheet". Then add each row and enter the total for each row in the right hand column.

The first number in each box is the question you answered, beside each number place the corresponding value (3= almost always / 2 = Often / 1 = Seldom / 0 = Rarely)

								Total Score	
1 /	14 /	27 /	40 /	53 /	66 /	79/	92 /		A
2 /	15 /	28 /	41 /	54 /	67 /	80 /	93 /		B
3 /	16 /	29 /	42 /	55 /	68 /	81 /	94 /		C
4 /	17 /	30 /	43 /	56 /	69 /	82 /	95 /		D
5 /	18 /	31 /	44 /	57 /	70 /	83 /	96 /		E
6 /	19 /	32 /	45 /	58 /	71 /	84 /	97 /		F
7 /	20 /	33 /	46 /	59 /	72 /	85 /	98 /		G
8 /	21 /	34 /	47 /	60 /	73 /	86 /	99 /		H
9 /	22 /	35 /	48 /	61 /	74 /	87 /	100 /		I
10 /	23 /	36 /	49 /	62 /	75 /	88 /	101 /		J
11 /	24 /	37 /	50 /	63 /	76 /	89 /	102 /		K
12 /	25 /	38 /	51 /	64 /	77 /	90 /	103 /		L
13 /	26 /	39 /	51 /	65 /	78 /	91 /	104 /		M

STEP THREE- transfer the totals from the "Response Sheet" to the list below to identify which letters correlates with each spiritual gift.

A =_____ Prophecy

B =_____ Evangelism

C =_____ Mercy

D =_____ Pastoring

E =_____ Service

F =_____ Giving

G =_____ Hospitality

H =_____ Teaching

I =_____ Exhortation

J =_____ Wisdom

K =_____ Leadership

L =_____ Administration

M =_____ Faith

UNWRAPPING MY GIFTS

The Bible does not lock us into tight restrictions as to the number of spiritual gifts, or even their definitions. The four major lists of gifts are found in Romans 12:3-8; 1 Cor. 12:1-11, 27-31; Eph, 4:11-12; and 1 Peter 4:9-11. However, there are other passages that mention or illustrate gifts not included in these lists.

Each list is different in order and content. This variation probably reflects the differing needs and conditions in the local congregation to which these passages were written. The Holy Spirit gives gifts according to specific need rather than all the gifts to all people and all churches.

Although there is no division scripturally that categorizes the gifts, for the sake of understanding we've categorized the gifts into three areas:

GIFTS THAT COMMUNICATE GOD'S LOVE AND TRUTH

PROPHECY (Preaching)   **1 Cor. 14:3**
The ability to publicly communicate God's Word in an inspired way that convinces, challenges and comforts people.

EVANGELISM   **Acts 8:26-40**
The ability to communicate the Good News of Jesus Christ to seekers in effective ways. The ability to sense opportunities to share Christ and lead people to respond with faith.

TEACHING   **Eph. 4:12-13**
The ability to educate God's people by clearly explaining and applying the Bible in a way that causes them to learn. The ability to equip and train other believers for ministry.

EXHORTATION (Encouragement)   **Acts 14:22**
The ability to motivate people to apply and act on biblical principles. To compel and encourage them to live in God's Will especially when they are discouraged or wavering in their faith.

WISDOM (Counseling)   **1 Cor. 2:1, 6-16**
The ability to understand God's perspective on life situations and share those insights in a simple, understandable way. The ability to listen effectively and assist people with what to do and how to do it.

DISCERNEMENT   **1 John 4:1-6**

The ability to distinguish right from wrong, truth from error and to give an immediate evaluation based on God's Word.

KNOWLEDGE   **Daniel 1:17**

The ability to discover, collect, analyze, and organize information that is vital to individual believers or the entire church family. The ability to comprehend a large amount of information and provide it when needed for effective decision-making.

GIFTS THAT DEMONSTARATE GOD'S LOVE AND TRUTH

SERVICE (Helps)   **Acts 6:1-7**

The ability to recognize unmet needs in the church family, and take the initiative to provide practical assistance quickly, cheerfully, and without a need for recognition.

MERCY   **Luke 10:30-37**

The ability to detect hurt and empathizes with those who are suffering in the church family. The ability to provide compassionate and cheerful support to those experiencing distress, crisis, or pain.

HOSPITALITY   **1 Peter 4:9-10**

The ability to make others, especially strangers, feel warmly welcomed, accepted, and comfortable in the church family. The ability to coordinate facets that promote fellowship.

PASTORING ("Shepherding")   **1 Peter 5:2-4**

The ability to care for the spiritual needs of a group of believers and equip them for ministry. The ability to nurture a small group in spiritual growth and assume responsibility for their welfare.

GIVING   **2 Cor. 8:1-7, Rom. 12:8**

The ability to generously contribute money and material resources beyond the 10% tithe to the work of the Lord with cheerfulness and liberality.

GIFTS THAT AUTHENTICATE GOD'S LOVE AND TRUTH

MIRACLES   **1 Cor. 12:10,28**
The ability to pray in faith specifically for God's supernatural intervention into an impossible situation and see God answer.

HEALING   **James 5:14-16**
The ability to pray in faith specifically for people who need physical, emotional or spiritual healing and seek God's answer to these needs.

PRAYING WITH MY SPIRIT (Tongues/Interpretation)
1Cor. 14:13-15
The ability to pray in a language understood only by God or by one who is given the gift of interpretation at that time.

FAITH   **Romans 4:18-21**
The ability to trust God for what cannot be seen and to act on God's promise, regardless of what the circumstances indicate. The willingness to risk failure in pursuit of a God-given vision, expecting God to handle the obstacles.

GIFTS THAT COORDINATE ALL THREE CATEGORIES

LEADERSHIP   **Hebrews 13:7, 17**
The ability to clarity and communicate the purpose and direction (vision) of a ministry in a way that attracts others to get involved. The ability to motivate others by example to work together in accomplishing a ministry goal.

ADMINISTRATION (Organization)   **1 Cor. 14:40**
The ability to recognize the gifts of others and recruit them to a ministry. The ability to organize and manage people, resources, and time for effective ministry. The ability to coordinate many details and execute the plans of leadership.

Gifts That <u>Communicate</u> God's Love And Truth
Prophecy (Preaching)
Teaching
Exhortation
Wisdom
Discernment
Knowledge

Gifts That Demonstrate God's Love And Truth
Service
Mercy
Hospitality
Pastoring
Giving

Gifts That Authenticate God's Love And Truth (Sign Gifts)
Miracles
Healing
Tongues/Interpretation
Faith

Gifts That Coordinate All Three Categories
Leadership
Administration

Section Two: Passions

Someone has defined a passion as anything you would find yourself doing if you had nothing else to do. In Christ, our passions (heart, motivations, calling, desires) can be used in powerful ways for the good of others and for the gospel of Christ.

Passion in Christ is where my heart meets someone else's need.

<u>We see Passions in different people in the Bible...</u>

Paul for the Gentiles (Romans 15:20)
Peter for the Jews (Galatians 2:7-8)
Luke for accuracy in the historical record of Jesus (Luke 1:1-4)
King David for music (1 Corinthians 15:6; 2 Chron. 7:6)
Jesus for Lost People (Matthew 9:12; Luke 19:10)

Keys to Discovering Passion:

1. Identify what gets you excited.

Ask yourself: 'What's important to me? What do I like to do? What or who do I really care about?"

2. Go back to your childhood.

One way to tell if something is your passion is if you had an affinity for it during childhood.

3. Take stock of your God-given gifts.

What you love is likely what you're gifted at.

4. Look at the big picture.

Do I like doing it? Am I gifted for it? Does the world need it?

PASSION ASSESSMENT:

1. What one subject can you enjoy talking about for a long time?

2. What do you naturally find yourself doing in your spare time?

3. What specific concerns preoccupy your mind that often interrupt whatever else you're thinking about?

4. What do you most enjoy doing for others?

5. Let's pretend you've reached the end of your life, and you're in heaven looking back on it. What's the one thing you want to be most happy about having done or having been?

6. Who 'out there' in the world have you come to care about the most? Who do you most want to help, enable, or reach? (You define the categories, whatever way you want. Go with your first instincts.)

7. Now, write down at least five of your life experiences that most gave you a sense of fulfillment and/or growth. (Don't think about them until later -- just write them down for now.) If more experiences come to mind, just keep listing them until you exhaust yourself. You'll sort them out later. (use back of sheet)

Final Question: Your "God smile" test.
What have you found yourself doing where you felt God's pleasure and peace in that you sensed what you were doing was important, and pleasing to God?

Section Three: Personality

Adult DISC Profile

Understanding yourself and others

For over thirty years, the *DiSC* behavioral profile has been available to assist people in understanding themselves and others. It has offered an easy-to-use, inexpensive, and popular vehicle for self development to participants and facilitators worldwide. The theoretical model on which this instrument is based comes from *Emotions of Normal People*, a 1928 publication by Dr. William Moulton Marston. Marston's Model was the basis for the original *DiSC Classic*, which was developed by researchers at the University of Minnesota in 1972.

Differences in Perception:

DISC BEHAVIOR SURVEY

Instructions: Focus on the instinctive behavior of someone you desire to better understand. Better yet let them complete the assessment.

How to respond: Rank each *horizontal* row of words on a scale of 4, 3, 2, 1 with 4 being the word that **best** describes you and 1 being the *least* like you. Use all rankings in each line *only* once. Below is an example:

[2] Dominant	[1] Influencing	[4] Steadiness	[3] Compliant
[ ] Forceful	[ ] Lively	[ ] Modest	[ ] Tactful
[ ] Aggressive	[ ] Emotional	[ ] Accommodating	[ ] Consistent
[ ] Direct	[ ] Animated	[ ] Agreeable	[ ] Accurate
[ ] Tough	[ ] People-oriented	[ ] Gentle	[ ] Perfectionist
[ ] Daring	[ ] Impulsive	[ ] Kind	[ ] Cautious
[ ] Competitive	[ ] Expressive	[ ] Supportive	[ ] Precise
[ ] Risk taker	[ ] Talkative	[ ] Gentle	[ ] Factual
[ ] Argumentative	[ ] Fun-loving	[ ] Patient	[ ] Logical
[ ] Bold	[ ] Spontaneous	[ ] Stable	[ ] Organized
[ ] Take charge	[ ] Optimistic	[ ] Peaceful	[ ] Conscientious
[ ] Candid	[ ] Cheerful	[ ] Loyal	[ ] Serious
[ ] Independent	[ ] Enthusiastic	[ ] Good listener	[ ] High standards
_____ Total	_____ Total	_____ Total	_____ Total
[ ]	[ ]	[ ]	[ ]

Note: If your totals do not add up to 120, you did not complete the survey correctly or you made a mistake in adding up the totals. Recheck your work.

Tallying Your Score:

1. On the previous page, enter the letter "D" in first large box; enter "I" in the second; "S" in the third; and "C" in the fourth.

Transfer the disc totals from the bottom of the previous page to the tally box below:

Tally Box:

D	I	S	C

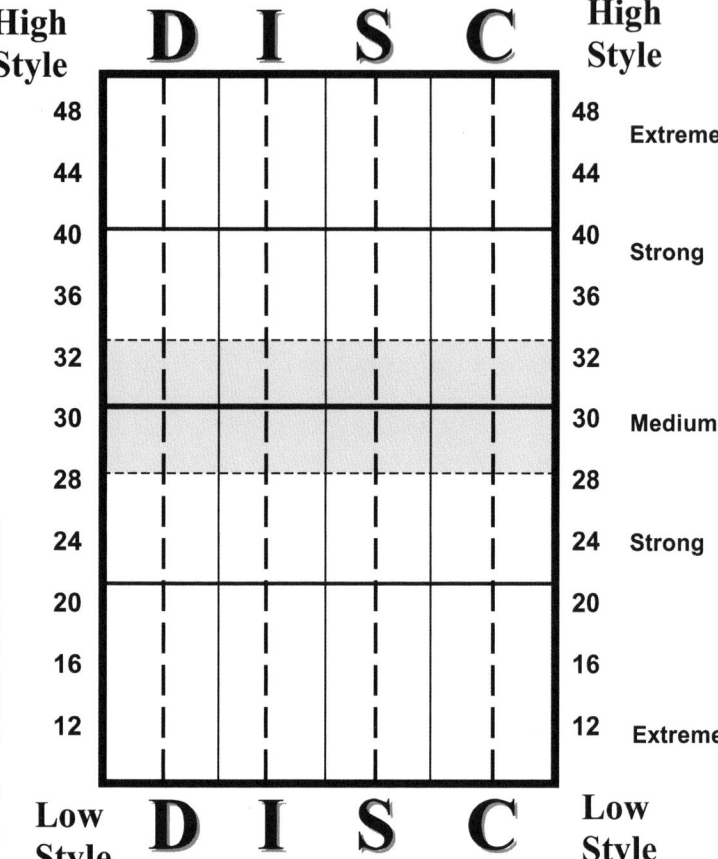

2. Using the totals from your tally box, plot your D-I-S-C dimensions on the graph to the right; then connect the four points.

3. After completing your graph, circle all plotting points above the midline.

My High Style(s) are: _____

4. Below are definitions of DISC styles.

- **Dominant Styles:** Work toward achieving goals and results; they function best in an active, challenging environment.

- **Influencing Styles:** Work toward relating to people through verbal persuasion; they function best in friendly, favorable, environment.

- **Steadiness Styles:** Work toward supporting and cooperating with others; they function best in supportive, harmonious environment.

- **Conscientious Styles:** Work toward doing things right and focus on details; they function best in a structured, orderly environment.

Assignment: Based on the information above, write a personalized definition:

I tend to work toward…

And function best in an environment that is…

Overview of DISC Styles

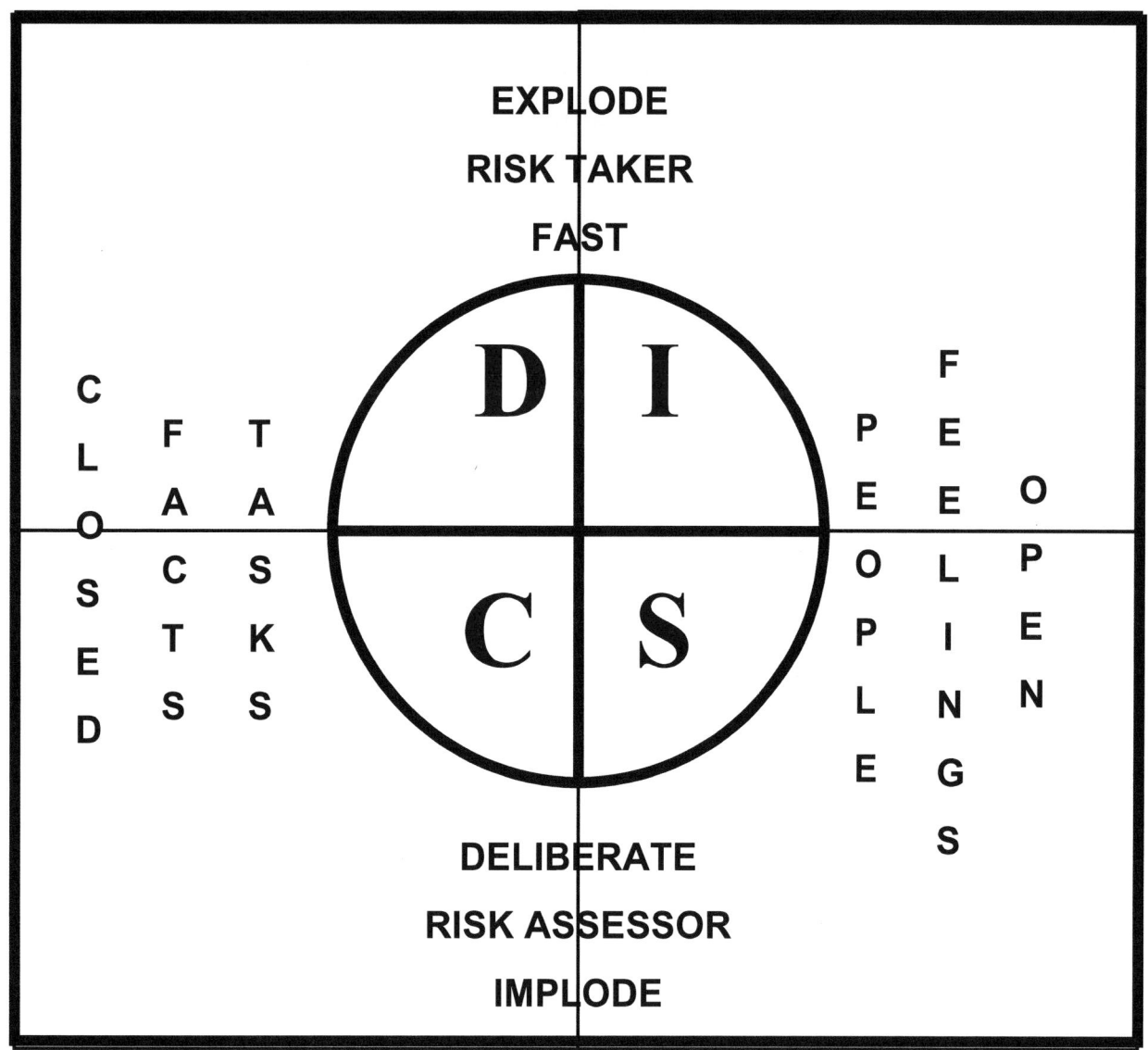

High D-
- *Tells more than asks*
- *Talks more than listens*
- *Forceful tone of voice*
- *Blunt and to the point*
- *Fast rate of speech*
- *Confident and decisive*
- *Speak about their results, goals, bottom lines.*

High I-

- *Tells stories and anecdotes*
- *Share personal feelings*
- *Speaks with emotion*
- *Animated facial expression*
- *High energy level*
- *Touches others when talking*
- *Smiles, laughs and talks with hands.*

High C-
- *Asks for clarification*
- *Does not share feelings openly*
- *Little inflection when speaking*
- *Deliberate, thoughtful, and unemotional in their communication*
- *Focuses on rules and regulations*
- *Formal and serious*
- *High attention to details*

High S-
- *Asks more than tells*
- *Listens more than talks*
- *Deliberate, but indirect in communication*
- *Slower moving*
- *Steady and warm tones in voice*
- *Patient and polite*
- *Sensitive to other's needs*

Understanding Your Basic Style

Action Plan: (Circle) the High & Low Types below that correspond with High & Low Styles on your graph on page 16. For understanding your Basic Style, take a few minutes to consider these Basic Style traits that you circled for *Act, Want, Fear* and *Response* in each of the High or Low types in your style. Do the traits accurately describe you?

High Type	D	I	S	C
Act	Assertive	Persuasive	Patient	Contemplative
Want	Control	Approval	Routine	Standards
Fear	Losing	Rejection	Change	Being Wrong
Response	Anger	Blame	Nonparticipation	Criticisms
Act	Cooperative	Unemotional	Responsive	Free-spirited
Want	Harmony	Logic	Variety	Non-structured
Fear	Confrontation	Illogical Act	Status Quo	Conforming
Response	Indifference	Suspicion	Physical Action	Emotion
High Type	D	I	S	C

Using the chart above, define your basic style by completing the statement below:

Defining Your Basic Style

As a/an _____ style blend, I naturally act _____
                                                                                                          act

because I want _____ .
                                                                                  want

If I perceive that I may face _____ ,
                                                                                      fear

I may respond with _____
                                                                                 response

Understanding Your Negotiating Style in Resolving Conflict

Action Plan: Again, (circle) the High & Low Types below that correspond with High & Low Styles on your graph on page 16. For understanding your Basic Style, take a few minutes to consider these Basic Style traits that you circled for *Comfortable, Fears, Tensions* and *Conflict* in each of the High or Low types in your style. Do the traits accurately describe how you handle conflict?

High Type	**D**	**I**	**S**	**C**
Comfortable	Decisive	Enthusiastic	Supportive	Structured
Fears	Losing	Rejection	Change	Being Wrong
Tension	Demands action	Emotional Attacks	Complies	Avoids Disagreeing
Conflict	Avoids conflict	Complies	Stubbornly	Demands
Comfortable	A Team Player	Detached	Spontaneous	Unstructured
Fears	Confrontation	Illogical Actions	Status Quo	Conforming
Tension	Becomes quiet	Remains calm	Challenges	Becomes
Conflict	Stuff feelings	Reacts covertly	Assesses	Becomes
High Type	**D**	**I**	**S**	**C**

Using the chart above, define your conflict style by completing the statement below:

Defining Your Basic Style

I am most <u>comfortable</u> being _____

When I feel <u>fears</u> of _____ it causes tension for me.

Under <u>tension</u> I may _____,

If this intensifies the <u>conflict</u>, I may _____

Printed in Dunstable, United Kingdom